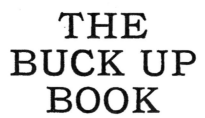

THE BUCK UP BOOK

BY

F. D. VAN AMBURGH

First Edition

PUBLISHED BY

THE SILENT PARTNER CO.

200 Fifth Avenue,

NEW YORK CITY

Printing Statement:

Due to the very old age and scarcity of this book, many of the pages may be hard to read due to the blurring of the original text, possible missing pages, missing text, dark backgrounds and other issues beyond our control.

Because this is such an important and rare work, we believe it is best to reproduce this book regardless of its original condition.

Thank you for your understanding.

TO

the Memory of Our Boys, and to those whose Self-Sacrificing Service and Devotion to Duty will live afresh in the ever-growing, never-aging Gratitude of all Americans.

CONTENTS

FOREWORD

IT was evening. A body bent with the trials of life — a man past middle age — had just forded a swift, swollen, uncertain stream; and when I saw him he was earnestly working, patiently building a footbridge out of driftwood — building a small span over the very stream he had just crossed.

And I said to him: "Friend, why do you build a bridge? You are safe on the other side. The evening of your Life is here. You will never retrace your steps. You must go on — on, Forever.

The old man, who had laid pontoon bridges for Posterity all his life, replied: "True, I never expect to go over this trail again; but, you know, I've a Son that's coming this way."

The author of this little work has been building bridges for years, Not for Posterity, but for People Present.

He has been trying to help his neighbor's son — the boy next door.

The author believes there are two trails in
Life. One trail leads along the foothills,
through the valley and down into the swamps
of Despair, where those who travel are forever looking over their shoulders in trembling
and fear.

The other trail, you will find, is higher up the
hill, and it leads to the very Apex of Ambition — up, up where the light lingers even
when the sun is down.

For years the trail of the author's Life led him
to the very crest of the mountain — left him
at an altitude often above the clouds.

Literally " living in the clouds " loans inspiration. It lifts the horizon of Hope and extends
the viewpoint.

And while he was living in the miracle of
mist that gathers over the great granite mountains of the marvelous West — while living in
silence and mystery — the author would often
awaken at dawn and watch with eagerness
the wavering lines of range after range that
resemble breakers on the shore.

You say: " Yes, the author is one of those
Optimists that lives in the clouds."

To have your feet on the rugged rocks and
still live in the clouds teaches one to be More
than an optimist.

If there be any virtue in the efforts of the
author, it is to produce a Sensible, Reasonable

book of Practical Philosophy and not Wild-Eyed Optimism.

Into the Life of every human, at some time, come sorrow, bitterness, disappointment, discouragement, doubt, perplexity, apprehension, fear, hate, envy, jealousy, self-pity — all demons of Thought.

Then illness and disease are likely to intrude and do all the damage permitted.

Life, under the baleful influences of these undesirable elements, becomes drab — colorless — hopeless — joyless; but, most of all, Useless.

Uselessness is a crime against oneself and against humanity.

In The Buck Up Book you will find many ways and means to eliminate these undesirable, these Deadly Elements; for The Buck Up Book is full of Hope — the hope that is founded on the Practical Philosophy of everyday, common-place living and doing.

The Buck Up Book will lead you away from the bogs, the low spots, lead you away from the marshlands of Life, up where the night sky is full of bright stars and where the day is clear and pleasant.

The whole idea in this book is to get you to look up, think up, brush up — to get you to Buck Up.

To get you to make an honest, a new and

clearer Analysis of Yourself, to help you to start on a New Trail, and to encourage you to Keep Going.

In this work the reader will find considerable space devoted to the Mind. The author believes the Mind is a wonderful healer or a decided destroyer, depending on the attitude of the Mind.

Hypodermics of pure water have put millions to sleep. Bread pills have performed almost miracles. Yet these truths do not for one instant discount the value of the conscientious physician, the dependable druggist; nor do they lessen the loyalty of the experienced nurse.

The author has tried to show the value of all valuable factors that get humans to Buck Up. Life is a battle of brains, and every Mind needs encouragement. The Buck Up Book is presented to the public, in a Crisis, to help men Up the Hill.

It introduces science, creeds and cults for the purpose of Adaptation — not for the plan of Adoption.

It will rely implicitly on the results one is reasonably sure to get from Hard Work, Horse Sense and Honest Purpose.

Edith M. Burtis.

KNOW THYSELF

This wise injunction, "Know Thyself," intimately concerns the reader. The subject was inspired by a personal acquaintance with John L. Mench.

Mix a lot of Will with a certain amount of Skill. Stir well, and take a big dose before you leave the house in the morning. If your system rebels at the treatment, you don't need medicine. What you want is a Swift Kick between the henhouse and the barn.

The Buck Up Book has been written to broaden your mind with the Ambition and Ability to investigate Systematically and Honestly all that comes under your observation in the life of others and particularly in your own life.

Common sense is not the result of education, it is in Spite of it.

THAT you may do your own Work well — Know Thyself. That you may work with others Successfully — Know Thyself.

A careful, conscientious measurement of Number One is absolutely necessary for success.

Until you know more of Yourself, little will you know of Others.

Until you can control yourself, manage yourself, you may expect a Small Salary for managing others.

Self-knowledge is the point where Wisdom centers.

Now that your mind is directed to a most important thought, let me warn you to love yourself Last.

So many men flatter themselves, fool themselves, believe that they are Exceptional.

The supreme fall of all falls is when a man Loves himself most.

Then again, a man can take a Terrible Tumble when he doubts himself.

The weak link in any man's life is the one that holds his head firmly with Personal Flattery — the link that chains him to the idea that he is very wise.

Why do men discover faults in other men so promptly and Perfection in themselves so surely?

Why is the average man a Small man?

Why is it that a man will acknowledge some one unimportant fault?

Is it a plan to overshadow some more serious personal Defect?

Is it a scheme to throw the flashlight in the other fellow's face?

Are you willing to come out, after reading this article and tell to the world your most flagrant faults?

I think not.

16

To acknowledge your weakness to the world,
after you have discovered it, is a Modesty too
much to expect of man.

To tell your faults to your friends is ingenuousness.

To preach to the world of your Faults is proof that you are out of the clutch of your Faults.

To be conscious of no fault in yourself is one of the Greatest individual faults in all the world.

The Buck Up Book has been written to broaden your mind with the Ambition and Ability to investigate Systematically and Honestly all that comes under your observation in the life of others and particularly in your own life.

Common sense is not the result of education, it is in Spite of it.

The grandest, the greatest education in all the world is to have the Common Sense, Disciplined by Experience, to study and Know Thyself.

The sun goes down at night and submits to being obscure.
But just as sure as the clock ticks at a certain moment in the morning, up comes the sun.
Mist and cloud may obscure the sun again, but in God's own way the sun is Sure to shine Somewhere.
When things look dark and discouraging, keep in mind the Regular Order of Events.

WILD-EYED OPTIMISM

It is better to be a bankrupt in sunshine than a millionaire in shadow. Better to be broke with your appreciation of living, than to be rich with the regret of having to wait for death

I believe that there is a bigger word, a better word, than Optimism. And it is — Courage.

OPTIMISM is said to be the sunshine of the soul.

The optimist seldom carries an umbrella, and you know it sometimes rains.

Years ago the author of this book lived on the desert of Disappointment and prospected for gold with a bunch of wild-eyed optimists. On the desert it was all sunshine.

My suggestion to you is to have little in common with the Optimist. He is at best a continuous performance of Hope.

The Optimist is like the wise old owl that can see only in the dark — that can see only while the normal man is supposed to be sleeping.

The Optimist is the theorist who transports you from a world of actuality into a paradise prepared for the tread of the fool.

The Optimist will clutch a straw and claim

21

he has caught a St. Croix River raft of white pine.

He gets all flushed up, gets all excited over colors that he finds in the prospector's pan — colors that prove to the experienced eye to be nothing but iron pyrites.

The Optimist believes that everything is bound to come out all right even without work. He says, to himself: " Let 'er slide." You say this is severe criticism on the Optimist and not well founded. Now, let us see if this criticism really lacks foundation.

Webster tells us that Optimism is " the doctrine that everything is ordered for the best." Now wouldn't this definition of optimism jar you?

In a former book written by the author of The Buck Up Book — a book called " By the Side of the Road "— you will find this significant sentence: " Between the Optimist who feels that he is sailing in a safe channel and the Pessimist who refuses to row — I say, between these two extremes in human nature, we have the Normal Man."

No! The Optimist has no charm for me. I have paid for his golden dream.

Optimism is founded on the belief of the Fatalist: " Everything is ordered for the best."

So, you see, we have misused the word Optim-

22

ism, or rather, misunderstood the word Optimism. Any belief that has every goose a
swan is beyond my power of comprehension.
I believe that there is a bigger word, a better
word, than Optimism. And it is — Courage.
Courage creates the resolute heart. Courage
understands that Life is bigger than any one
battle. Courage intelligently contemplates all
obstacles.

Years ago there was a knocker on the front
door. Later it required a pull at the door-
bell to attract attention. To-day you punch
an electric button.

The knocker is out of date. A pull is passé.
It now takes an electrified punch. That is
why I take issue with the late Senator Ingalls
and his verse, " Opportunity "— Opportunity
that knocks but once.

The only way you can get the door of Opportunity open is to Push, not knock.

A smile is the Passport to Prosperity.
It promotes business; and incidentally
business is an important occupation.
Besides the profits we find that follow a
smile, there is a lot of satisfaction in Living a pleasant life.

CLEANNESS

Cleanness: a thought suggested by E.
St. Clair.
The impertinence, the impudence of expression should be charged to the author
and not to Mr. St. Clair.

Rivet this fact in your brain box: No man can gain success and stay a success without the public is with him. All men are public servants, and for this reason they occupy a public trust.

When the public loans a man success, it is because he Deserves it.

The great value of education, the wonderful worth of ambition — both advantages suffer Defeat in the presence of a personality that lacks Cleanness.

CLEANNESS of personality is a Certificate of Character.

There are exceptions to all rules, and this rule is no exception.

Humans who have a due reverence for God, for society and for themselves are almost always conspicuous for their Cleanness.

The off-scum, the hog-wash, the dandruff-dirty of society are always in the dependent class.

The grimy, the filthy and the soiled fill our Prisons.

The untidy, uncombed, unclean accept our Charity.

Personal appearance has a lot to do with a man's chances in life. When a man gets smutty and dusty, folks will Sidestep him.

Let your teeth get overlaid with yellow moss, the back of your neck covered with untrimmed underbrush, your finger nails uneven and banked with greased mud, let your shoes get sloppy and your trousers frayed at the bottom, and Nobody Wants You.

Remember this: Ambition will not dwell with Dirt. Virtue will not remain Unwashed. So long as the rivers run and the scavengers gather soap grease, there is Hope.

I know men personally who pretend to be respectable, and to a degree they are responsible. But these men, when they get warmed up, smell like a basket of Soiled Linen. They are actually Dirty. When they remove their collars in the barber shop you can see the black streaks around their necks. They get shaved almost every day, and this is the Extent of their washing — from the neck up. The cost or the cut of a suit of clothes cannot compensate for the easily obtainable requirement — Cleanness. A silk shirt on a dirty man will not answer as a passport. It looks like a morning gown on a razor-back hog in the hills of Arkansas.

The great value of education, the wonderful worth of ambition — both advantages suffer Defeat in the presence of a personality that lacks Cleanness.

28

MOTHER

No silver can compare with a Mother's soft white hair. No lines are half so beautiful as those in the furrowed face of your Mother. No sculptor can dream of such beauty as in those patient hands. When you go home to-night, take this storm-tossed soul close to your big heart, and say the things you would want her to know if she were resting in the front room, with sunken, sightless eyes, and cold, white lips.

Give her a Rosary of Kind Words now! She will count them over a dozen times to-morrow.

It is at a Mother's grave that one finds more outward things and more inward thoughts teeming with assurances of immortality than any other place on earth.

IF it were possible for the writer to pluck the rarest flowers of rhetoric, the handsomest roses in all remembrance of thought, I would fashion, in one Crown of Love and Affection, the most Beautiful Tribute in all the world, and place it tenderly on the brow of — Mother.

If it were possible for me to paint on the canvas of sentiment the most marvelous event since the infant King in the starlit Manager of Bethlehem, it would be a scene where God opens the Great Gate and gives to the world that Wonderful Woman — Mother.

In the past, men, in their pressing march for position or prosperity, have often neglected their Dearest Friend on earth — Mother.

Men in their Mad Rush for Money have forgotten to take a little time and cheer the few remaining days of Mother.

But this war has changed the whole situation. Men are beginning to understand better the value, the incomparable Gift of a Mother's presence in the Home.

Did I say, " Men are beginning to understand better "? No! They are beginning to understand themselves better.

From to-day on there will be room for but One Queen in this world, and that queen will be — Mother.

Your Mother may be bent in body, trembling in thought, but she is your Mother — she is the same sacrificing, devoted, dear old Mother that you loved so when you were a boy.

Her opinions of things may not always sound scientifically correct, but you may rest assured that her thoughts are morally right.

She may venture some old-fashioned idea in preference to some modern method, and her plans may look like the longer way round, but you will find they are the Sure way.

Can't you remember when your Mother used to clean and cook for you, and how she darned your stockings and mended your ball? Can you recall the times when she would get up at night and cover your restless body with the quilt that she made by hand, and how she listened for your croupy cough? Of course you can't, but she did this a Thousand Times. When you were a boy she had time to listen

32

to your fairy tales. At least, she took the
time. Are you willing to listen to her now?
Can you remember when you started out for
your first job? Who smiled and helped you
on the way? Who was the last one to say
some encouraging word? — Mother.
She probably did without dresses that you
might appear before your fellows unashamed.
On the pillow of this wonderful woman's
breast you have slept, and from her Life you
have Lived.
Over your life to-day hangs this high and pure
Guiding Star, even though you may be com-
pelled to listen for her voice through the long
corridor of receding years.
The Potential Power of the American army is
— Mother.
The Rock on which Humanity must rest is —
Mother.
The one word that brings back all that is best
in All of us is — Mother.
Mother! Your heart loaned the pulsations of
my heart. My soul is but part of your soul.
My body is but part of your dear body.
Mother! You incomparable, you Wonderful
Woman — you mercy of God.
Life may loan to us all so many beautiful
things: roses, rainbows, sunsets in thousand
lots, stars by the tens of thousands — life may
loan us a dear old Dad, faithful brothers, sym-

pathetic sisters and friends by the score —
but never, never but once will life loan us a
Mother!

How the thoughts of this individual creation of
God differs from all His other earthly gifts!

No matter how much trouble may come to
you to-day, think how patiently and lovingly
your Mother would untangle the threads —
think with what infinite patience she played
her part — her important part.

Not long ago I stood in the Silence of my
Mother's grave. The radiant moon sent its
silver-toned shadows across the green, low
mound. The spring rains had washed away
the snows of winter, and all about were the
season's transfiguration.

It is at a Mother's grave that one finds more
outward things and more inward thoughts
teeming with assurances of immortality than
any other place on earth.

It was at my Mother's grave, in a simple little
churchyard back in the country, that I could
see the light of an Endless Day.

RIGHT ENTHUSIASM

There are different degrees of enthusiasm, different brands.
The author feels that M. L. Parker has selected the best brand —" Right Enthusiasm."

You will find that the figures that will foretell the total of your coming success are in proportion to your present interest in some one line of work or profession.

Your desire to excel in some one line is sure to stimulate you to more action, inspire you to do better Work.

Your success does not depend wholly on your ability, but it depends a lot on the particular Job you pick out to do.

One can find the job that fits him sooner than he can conform to the Requirements of the job.

My suggestion is this: Find the job that fits you, that will furnish sufficient incentive for you to do your Level Best. See that the job offers plenty of Opportunity. Satisfy yourself that the job needs You. Then take hold of the job with both hands; get back of the job with both feet; put your heart, your head and your every hope in the thing, and then Do the thing.

You seldom see a man that is full of gimp
and go, full of the fire of Right Enthusiasm,
after he has reached the third degree of calm
and calculating prosperity.

IGHT ENTHUSIASM is the
biggest and the best brand.
Right Enthusiasm is intoxi-
cated individual interest; and
this intimately personal interest must be established by
Necessity, that one may win permanently anything worth while.

Enthusiasm of the ordinary kind is bounded
on the north by Ambition, on the east by Desire, on the south by Hope, and on the west
by Passion.

Right Enthusiasm is bounded on the north,
east, south and west by Necessity.

Right Enthusiasm gives a man the punch, the
prod, the real reason for having to go on.

It puts a new point on a bayonet in the battle of business. It puts a new slant on success. It concerns all the points of compass in
our calculations.

Right Enthusiasm is the enthusiasm born of having to Do.

You say — and I have often said —" What we want in others in a disposition to want to do." The man who must do and then fails to do will probably never want to do.

You seldom see a man that is full of gimp and go, full of the fire of Right Enthusiasm, after he has reached the third degree of calm and calculating prosperity.

The Enthusiasm of Necessity is the answer to a fear of adversity.

It is a lucky thing for you and for me that we have to hike, otherwise we would lie on our lazy backs under an apple tree, with our mouths wide open, and wait for the fruit to fall.

What a world this would be if we were all permitted to slack! Many would slack.

Duty is not nearly so strong as Necessity.

Necessity must Do things. Duty is often asleep at the switch.

Necessity knows no way out. It is the spur that has goaded great men.

The iron hand of Necessity commands; her stern decree is supreme.

Fortunate indeed is the human that must Do things. Unfortunate is the man that has money enough to be idle. Money makes too large a catalogue for the things a man wants.

38

When Necessity hoops in a man's Hopes and,
through many experiments, he touches on every side until he learns the arc of his possi-
bilities, then and not until then have you a
safe, a sensible, a secure man.

The point is, Found your Enthusiasm Right,
for the greatest dejection follows a fever of
Wrong Enthusiasm.

No man can play feverishly, pay extravagantly,
waste his resources at night, and then come to
the office, the store, the plant, in the morning
with what is called Right Enthusiasm — even
though necessity knocks, prods, pushes or
pulls.

Debauch, extravagance, waste of time only
add more load to Necessity.

For this very reason, Right Enthusiasm is
quite as much a physical as a mental prod-
uct.

What an awful load Necessity must carry
when it has to tote the lazy, shiftless, indiffer-
ent man!

What a punch behind the individual that
knows he Must!

You say to yourself, and sometimes to others: "Never mind; I'll win to-morrow."

And to-morrow you say the same thing. You make new designs, but the effort is not continuous. Then you make New Failures.

By and by the time of designing is Past. And here we face the terrible truth — the time of designing is Past!

WHAT I CALL POVERTY

My ambition is not to get where I can
take it easy.
My desire is to continue to have the fun
of doing things.
I am glad to get away from the office
at 5, and always eager to come in the
morning at 8:30.
It is not my prayer to have a task equal
to my power.
My hope is always to have Power equal
to my Task.
The true source of Genuine Happiness
is accomplishing something Worth While.
Arriving is the End.

I would rather see a man storm heaven itself
in his folly than witness a living dead one of
despair mourn at the mound of Past Mistakes.

HE colossal error of life is for one to get discouraged. It is either the conclusion of the sick, the abandonment of ambition, the rule of the reckless or the fate of the Fool.

To get discouraged is to invite your own house to fall on your own head. It is to add another Handicap.

When we contemplate the unforeseen future, when we consider the many pleasant hours of the past, what right have we to be discouraged or to get the blues?

Nothing could make the writer give up except the open page of the book that will record the hour of his death. And even then, if he were plowing, he would continue to plow.

Why wait for death?

If you have failed to insure your life, to make your will, to provide for your Family, to protect your bank, you are speculating with the chances against you.

Getting blue argues a defective spirit, a laziness of resolution. It is an evidence that you need a long march.

No one has any use for the bilious-looking individual. The world has no place for the Quitter, the Slacker, the Discouraged.

To-day it's go ahead or get off the trail. It's keep up or keep down. It's Sink or Swim.

The world from to-day on will be saved by Hope.

From to-day on, the discouraged, depressed, the down-in-the-mouth individual will receive small sympathy in the presence of the brave. A well man, a young man, will get a swift kick in the slats and be told to go to work.

We will reserve our sentiments and sympathy for soldiers who have Served.

And it is my suggestion here that everybody, everywhere, separate the man that Serves from the man that slacks. It is my suggestion that you steer clear of the discouraged, for they paralyze action.

From to-day on, the world will look with favor on the man that will look up, think up, Buck Up — the man that goes on like the torrent, never looking back.

I would rather see a man storm heaven itself in his folly than witness a living dead one of despair mourn at the mound of Past Mis- takes.

Men who shiver, tremble, shudder and shake over the future; men who hesitate, falter and flunk over the reverses of to-day, will find little consolation or pity to-morrow.

The Buck Up Book believes in placing an object before the reader, and the object is this — Poverty.

The inevitable consequence of being poor is Dependence.

Poverty is the one secure thing in society.

To have nothing in the way of cash is not what I call Poverty.

To Be Nothing is Poverty.

What men Hope to get is what seems to make men Happy. What men have and hold is the cause of most misery. We all see in the past the happiest hours in our lives, and most of us look upon the future with anxiety, albeit with enthusiasm. All of us look upon the Present as full of Trouble.

Not one man in twenty is happy over to-day. Happiness is a Habit that can be Acquired by a bit of right thinking, by a little Practical Philosophy.

When you realize that life is worth more than all else, and that to-day holds for you more of life than does to-morrow, you should appreciate more fully to-day.

HOPE SEES A STAR

Self-Directed action, self-governed intelligence, self-satisfied conscience — and here you have a man who will help himself and Help Others.

"But in the night of death Hope sees a star,
and listening Love can hear the rustling of a
wing."

ITH all the force and audacity
of his splendid oratory, Robert
G. Ingersoll opposed Chris-
tianity, attacked the Bible, and
questioned the existence of a
hell and the personal nature of
Deity. And for his thoughts, put in lecture
form, he was well paid.

Then Time led this man to the shut gate of
Life, and there he stood, on a beautiful day in
June, barred from his brother by the pitiless,
inexorable hand of Death.

Words that he had used before must have
fallen back into his heavy heart. A sense of
Isolation must have shrouded his soul, for out
of the depths of doubt we find him breathing
this beautiful tribute to Hope:

" Life is a narrow vale between the cold and
barren peaks of two eternities.

" We strive in vain to look beyond the heights.

49

"We cry aloud, and the only answer is the echo of our wailing cry.

"From the voiceless lips of the unreplying dead there comes no word.

"But in the night of death Hope sees a star, and listening Love can hear the rustling of a wing.

"He who sleeps here, when dying, mistaking the approach of death for the return of health, whispered with his latest breath, 'I am better now.'

"Let us believe, in spite of doubts and fears, that these dear words are true of all the countless dead."

Let a man's soul lack the spirit of Hope and the man, to all practical purposes, for all business requirements, is a lost cause.

If it were possible for a man to see the low mound and the fresh dirt, he would cry for help, for Hope.

Men live and defy Hope, and just before they die, they deplore their lack of common foresight.

WHITE CROWS

The master word of the world is "W-o-r-k." In the grasp of all great successes, you will see the rod of Energy and Efficiency.

Work is the schoolmaster of success. Education is bound in textbooks. Knowledge is education melted down into the button of experience. And you know it is experience that men want and are willing to pay for.

The mentally slow man will be quickened by Work. The common, everyday man will develop into the big man through Work. The brilliant mind is made steady by Work. Work fits all classes to be more Fit.

The writer of this work is your friend in disguise. The frankness of the book may lessen your warmth of heart toward the author, but if you learn from its pages the lesson of Individual Responsibility, the book will be a success so far as You are concerned.

 THE grandest possible Individual Incentive is to be awake to Personal Responsibility.

Hand in hand with every human should walk the Three Degrees of Personal Worth — Capacity, Power and Responsibility.

Your conscience must dictate the Duties you have to perform, the work you have to do.

The point is, awaken your Conscience. Put a Scotch thistle under your personal Responsibility to self and to society.

The Buck Up Book is intended to stimulate by a swift kick and not by pleasing platitudes.

It matters comparatively little how much you like the Author. It matters much what you think of Yourself.

The writer of this work is your friend in disguise. The frankness of the book may lessen your warmth of heart toward the author, but if you learn from its pages the lesson of Individual Responsibility, the book will be a success so far as You are concerned.

The whole thought of the author is to Construct by criticism and not destroy by condemnation.

If the book hits you where it hurts, be a good sport and take your medicine!

The worst enemy that you can encounter is the Flatterer. The best friend that you can find is the one who frankly reveals your faults. How true it is: A wise man flatters the weak, a fool flatters himself, a friend tells you the truth. Let me give you the Truth.

You are where you are by what you are. Had you been a bigger and a better man, you would now be miles and miles ahead. You are Responsible for your results.

Luck, Faith, Opportunity, Destiny — these White Crows have had nothing to do with your present position.

Small men believe in the shallow word Luck. Strong men believe in Cause and Effect.

The worst form of slavery is imposing upon your own neck the strict belief of Fate. The stoic believes in the unalterable course of events, and this is a Fatal courage.

Opportunity — and here is the word that you
think will stick me — Opportunity is the thing
a Wise man makes good in right where the
Fool fell flat.

Destiny! A birth star but not a fixed star.
Witness: St. Helena. Destiny is what Fate
imposes, so they say; and if this be true, why
try?

How silly for a man to depend on Destiny!
How weak a man must be that relies on empty
Chance, or what we call "Opportunity"!
How primitive the mind that measures all the
Future by the yardstick of Fate! How imma-
ture the brain that builds on the sands of the
shore a palace of Luck!

Results worth while are the answers to Intelligent Industry, Honest and Efficient Effort.

If you would have permanent success you
must necessarily think up, look up, Buck Up.
It is my claim that men and women do not
work hard enough. To Brutify action is not
to work. Automatic effort is but Slavery.

What I mean by work is Coöperation of head,
hands and heart. The mind must coöperate
with the muscles to bring out the Best.

Even though you rest your body, keep your
brain headed in the right direction and keep
it Working.

The human who regards an effort as mere

55

work will never rise higher than his two hind legs will support him.

You were not made for work: work was made for you.

Work is the most natural, normal thing in the world to do.

Until you like your Work and elect to excel, until you look upon your Work as a Real Opportunity to get away eventually from small service, until you enter the contest of Life to Win, you will always Work.

This is why I say: Keep Busy.

When humans are idle, they think of so many things that hinder! The nurse of naughtiness is nothing-to-do-until-to-morrow.

When a woman's mind or a man's mind is not on knitting, the probabilities are the woman or the man will get Morbid or Merry.

Let a man get out of work, and he will soon find where the Fools are holding a holiday.

It is almost impossible for a human to be Honest, Poor and Idle all in the same breath.

HOW FAR WILL YOU GO?

Men develop. John D. Rockefeller was a clerk. But instead of spending all his energy in trying to fool the boss, he devoted his best efforts to trying to Be the boss. He did not stick to sticking postage stamps on envelopes, or opening oil wells; but he set about to construct a perfect organization, a smooth corporation of muscle and of Mind; an organization that would work when he was not watching. He developed. If you are laying brick, keeping books, selling goods, you have the same chance to develop — probably better chances than many men. Lincoln left the log cabin. Garfield trudged on the towpath. Your boss probably started where you are — probably below where you are. Remember, in trying to fool the boss, you fool Yourself.

NO man will go past the point where he thinks he will.

When a man thinks he can't, he stops. When he decides he will, he usually goes ahead; and he continues to go ahead until his mind hesitates or halts, and then the distance seems far enough.

There is not a line in this book intended to Create Courage. The entire book has one special purpose — to Encourage Courage.

The American people have plenty of courage — all they require is recognition.

You like to have your work appreciated, and you are but one of one hundred millions.

So you see the idea of Encouraging Courage is a big one!

Before you start out on the trail of life, let me call you back and fortify you with this important thought: Success is half-brother to a bunch of blunders.

In other words, in perfectly plain words, when you feel disappointed over some expensive mistake, why get discouraged?

Until you make mistakes you will never know how, when or where to steer clear of mistakes. You do not want to know where the rocks are. You want to know where the rocks are not. You do not want to sail over rocks. You want to sail in the channel.

When a responsibility has been heavy enough, when an emergency has been great enough, when a motive has been large enough to call out the best in Americans, history has had another opportunity of recording some great result.

I repeat, we do not need to Create Courage — we need to Encourage Courage.

What The Buck Up Book is trying to accomplish is a mental method of Neutralizing Discouragement.

Everyone is sure to experience a mental depression, an hour when hope drops, when the idea of a bright future looks drab and dull.

Humans must have, at times, some bigger conception, some brighter possibility put before them.

Few, very few, can carry the extra load of a

trying day without looking backward to some stimulating sentiment, or looking forward to some inspiring Hope.

The power of expecting something, or the memory of having had something, is the spark plug that starts us on again after we feel that we cannot go another peg.

The point is, when you are blue, get your mind off the present as rapidly as you can. Think of the things worth Working for, worth Living for.

There are so many Wonderful things in this world, right now worth fighting for — Life, Love, Success, Home and the Dear Ones in it. You are no slacker — brace up, look up, Buck Up!

During our late artillery argument with the South, a certain man called at the White House and asked President Lincoln for a pass to Richmond.

Lincoln looked up, smiled, and then said: "I should like to help you, but, you see, I have been trying for two years to pass two hundred and fifty thousand men to Richmond."

Eventually the man reached Richmond, and you ask me how. The man joined the Army and Marched with his comrades to the city of his Ambition.

The power to do, the patience to endure, can only be acquired by Hard Work.

Work is the pledge of a comfortable old age, the guarantee of a decent middle life.

A common perversion of the truth is the statement that man is a slave to work. On the contrary, man would be a slave to some base practice without work.

Occupation, employment, business — these are the things that keep you out of mischief.

Every time that I have nothing to do, I find something to do that harms me.

FEAR FEAR

Fear, the tremendous, immense, marvel-
ous monster, whose eye is out.
Herbert P. Pearson has taught me that
Fear is but a tax levied on the weak.

You have probably watched a one-armed boy play ball; you have undoubtedly seen a one-legged man in a foot race; but neither of these handicapped humans is a Champion. What is holding You back?

Just as soon as you begin to worry, just as soon as you begin to fear something, apply the Antidote. Appeal to the same great law to which the Origin of Fear is due — the law of Self-Preservation.

EAR begins at babyhood and tugs at us all through life. Fear is the earliest instinct.

Fear is a painful emotion and produces a primitive agitation. This truth is what prompted Emerson to say: "Fear always comes from ignorance."

I would not be so foolish as to advise you to whistle in order to keep away fear, or to laugh that you may avoid some soul-chilling terror. It is Human to fear.

But this is not the fear that I am trying to feature.

One of the Deadliest things in life is Dread, Apprehension, Alarm. These words, in comparison with "soul-chilling terror," seem small; but remember this: we have dread with us all the time. We go "over the top," do some thrilling thing, but once or twice in a lifetime.

To fear a situation in business, in life, is but Foresight. To fear everyday things is to be Fortified.

You have lived so long, and the bugaboo of fear has not put you off the map.

When the nightmare of fear, when the hobgoblin of alarm, when the ghost of scare give you a great sinking spell, let me tell you why:

When you get all worked up over some business situation; when things look like indelible indigo; when everything seems to be going out and nothing coming in; when you get panicky, perplexed; when you are actually Afraid, you probably have Good Reason to be afraid.

When you fear something, there's a Reason. A good man never gets panicky over the loss of a paper of pins.

The logic that teaches that a man should not fear springs from the brain of a bug.

It is all foolishness, silly rot, to say that a man should not fear. The biggest and best business men in the world get panicky at times.

To fear is a natural sequence to success. To be able to meet fear face to face and knock its block off is possible.

Let me tell you how:

66

Just as soon as you begin to worry, just as
soon as you begin to fear something, apply the
Antidote. Appeal to the same great law to
which the Origin of Fear is due — the law of
Self-Preservation.

Bring yourself to understand that fear is sure
to damage you physically; and just as soon
as you get this fact firmly fixed in your top-
piece the mind will throw off fear.

Fear, in other words, is instantly avoided the
moment you fear Fear.

The Buck Up Book does not elect to tell you
how to do. It does aspire to get you to Want
to do.

The best way to get a man or a woman to want
to do is to reason of the advantages of doing a
thing worth while.

Voltaire says: "Systems exercise the mind,
but faith enlightens and guides it."

Let us exercise the mind a little on the subject
of Fear.

Men frequently take a tonic for the body; and
you know that there are more strong bodies
than there are powerful minds.

The author speaks from a personal experience — from an intimate knowledge of this
Truth.

With all my unbounded energy, with all my
unlimited enthusiasm, I frequently find it nec-

essary to read something bracing — to take a Mental Tonic.

When the thoughts of failure come creeping into my mind, when the poison of doubt or the epidemic of indifference gets hold of my old think-tank, out I go into the field of fresh thought with a Book, with a Friend or with the Flowers.

When doubt gets a grip on your mind, on your mental make-up, refuse to listen to the theory of possible failure.

In the event of your feeling discouraged, remember this: Be positive in your thoughts of success. Say to yourself: " I will! " Never let the little word " try " be added to the absolute, unqualified, positive statement " I will."

You exercise your body to make it strong. The same rule applies to the mind. Every time you say " I will," you create a new Mental Force.

When you say " I will try," you acknowledge to the world that you are weak in your belief that you will.

The point is, Fear Fear.

WHAT IS COURAGE?

We read of the imposing march of a mighty army, of the roar and the explosion, of the clatter of cavalry — we read of men who have risen to the full height of a public occasion; but stories of the lonely sentinel remain unsung.

Two thousand years ago, when nature was in revolt, when Cæsar's own army could not check the convulsions of a Higher Power, there stood, 'mid the volcanic ashes that were falling thick as the snowflakes, a lonely sentinel.

And when the granite archways of the great, Roman buildings tumbled, he remained at his post. Rushing past him were the citizens. But the servant of the people remained to fill orders.

Recently they uncovered the petrified, peerless, lonely sentinel. For two thousand years he stood beneath the ruins of a Roman city — stood on Guard!

There are sentinels at sea, sentinels in the mines, sentinels on the railroads, in the shops — sentinels of a home — and these posts call for the same Fortitude, the same Courage, the same Loyalty to the Legion of Honor!

No matter how humble your position, Stick to your Post!

OURAGE is many-sided; and this leaves room for the question: "What is Courage?" On investigation, this question will prove a subject worthy of careful analysis.

There is one brand of Courage that we all recognize. It faces front, goes forward, and calls: "Come on!"

Then there is the opposite form of human frailty, and we call it Fear.

Fear paralyzes purpose, gets wounded in the back, falls to the earth on its face and there gets in a good man's way.

The next form of Courage worthy of consideration is that Courage which Obeys the Organization, that endures and makes money for employer and employee.

The next form of Courage is that of Cheerfulness, Hope and Patience of the parents, wives and sweethearts, in their efforts to keep the home fires burning brightly.

71

But the Courage that commands our silent and special approval is what is called " Moral Courage."

Moral Courage comes from Resolve and Reason.

The Courage that resents some personal insult, some individual injury, is an everyday brand.

The Courage that will only march when cheered by the crowd is common and at last is but cowardice.

Let us emphasis Moral Courage.

Recently two American soldiers were captured a few hours before their company took a small town.

Naturally the American commander was deeply concerned in what would happen to these boys, and intensely interested in their absolute secrecy.

You know what happens, in this world war, to a captured soldier boy who has important information.

The American commander, knowing his two boys, assumed that they would be game. It is evident that they died with the truth under their tongues.

Being firm in a just cause while the cold, pointed steel is being pressed into your body is Moral Courage.

I consider the act of these two boys one of

72

the independent sparks from the very Throne of Moral Courage.

The Souls of these two soldiers, wherever they may be, go marching on.

The Buck Up Book would fail in its purpose should the subject of Courage end here.

The authors' ambition is to inspire individuals, to Encourage Courage to go onward and upward.

And the way to get men and women to go forward is to reason with them with reference to getting discouraged.

To have a weakening of confidence, to get the blues, to be dejected, to get discouraged, is human, perfectly human.

Discouragement is as necessary to man as a thunderstorm is to air. All success — and we would all be balloonists.

Since the beginning of the world, it has so happened to humans that every man has had his adverse seasons, his opposite hours.

When discouragement holds out its cold, hard hand — when its voice speaks with its stern, harsh note — all you can do, all you probably will do, is to let discouragement have the floor.

It is natural, normal, to get discouraged; but don't let the season of discouragement stick around too long.

73

Another thing: If there is anybody to witness your weakness, brace up, Buck Up.

Suffer in silence in order that you may not spill the beans for the other fellow. Smile like the cat that swallowed the robin.

Every human owes respect to the rights and interest of other humans, of society, of family and of the organization of which he or she is a member.

What right have you to let your mental condition warp the minds of others?

If you refuse to Buck Up, cheer up, keep up for your own sake, Buck Up for the sake of others.

THE BABY

New moral motives, new business aims
follow the arrival of the Baby. Every
letter I get from Clarence J. Strouss begins and ends with a thought of "The
Baby."

A little boy was playing in the street, the other day, when some one inquired of him: "Say, boy, don't you ever get angry?"

The lad looked up and replied: "I try not to get mad, 'cause when I do I don't have so much fun."

A baby will make love stronger, days shorter,
nights longer, bank rolls smaller, Home Happier, clothes shabbier, the past forgotten and
the future Worth Living For.

 OME women look upon a new-
born baby with strange and in-
explicable emotions.

Some women look upon a little
two-day-old tot with envy of
possession. For, you know,
the Bravest Battle has been fought by the
women that have lived Alone.

I have seen a bachelor look upon the face of a
baby with an offer in his countenance of a million dollars if he could honorably own the kid.
The baby is a peculiar little bundle. It speaks
no language and still it is a native of all coun-
tries.

The baby has been described as two feet of
coo and wriggle, scream and twist, filled with
suction and testing apparatus for milk, and an
automatic alarm to regulate supply.

We kiss a baby, and then we look around to

impress others with our capacity to love. Silently we wipe off the slobber.

The baby is a World Necessity, a nuisance for neighbors, and the one thing that will make a house a home.

The baby employs more female help than any other human. It lives in Lapland and can be heard almost any night as far as Scotland.

A baby will make love stronger, days shorter, nights longer, bank rolls smaller, Home Happier, clothes shabbier, the past forgotten and the future Worth Living For.

ANN HATHAWAY'S HUSBAND

Ann Hathaway's husband is a subject
that should put wings to several valuable thoughts.
"To live in our vital individuality," J. J.
Goldman says, "means much."

Each day I thank my lucky stars that I am compelled to Work. Should success sentence me to retirement, I should be a Most Miserable Man.

The world, in its coming centuries, will have time in which to make discoveries, but you, my friend, have none too much time in which to become Worth Discovering.

NN HATHAWAY, at the age of twenty-six, married a boy of eighteen. The lad was the son of English parents who could neither read nor write. At the age of fifty-two, Ann's husband died. This was three hundred and two years ago.

When Ann Hathaway's husband died, the greatest Genius of our world died.

The Intellectual Miracle of all time, the sage and seer of human nature, died.

Then was buried the greatest Moral Philosopher since the two Testaments.

And still, in the little town where this man lived he was scheduled as a Servant. Some folks were so small as to call him " A Sturdy Vagabond."

From this man the world received its richest rewards in Thought and in Action.

In all his many-colored views of writing, it never once occurred to him to construct a thought in which a wife's lover should be jealous of her husband. And, you know, this man was constantly writing of wives, husbands and sweethearts.

In all his works he was himself lost to view. His characters lived and died, with all the virtues and vices, with all the fears, hopes and hatreds, with all the customs, theories and superstitions of the human brain and the human heart.

Out of the unfathomable depths of his marvelous mind he supplied the world with advance thoughts that will march miles and miles Ahead of the coming centuries.

What he said then is more than true now, and will be forever and forever true to Nature and to Human nature.

The power of his invention made borrowing from the writers who had lived before him quite unnecessary. He did not write from rule, but his writing now stand as the rule.

By his noble extravagance of fancy he led the superstitious reader's imagination far past the support of reason and into the presence of ghosts and their solemn speeches.

This Supermind that belonged to Ann Hathaway's husband knew every cavern and every

cliff of the brain, knew all the currents and
tides of the Human Heart. He knew men,
women and their silent partners better than
they knew themselves.

In " Antony and Cleopatra " one can see the
slow-moving Nile run through the theme.
Even the great Sphinx casts its shadow over
the sands.

In " Julius Cæsar " the Eternal City rises from
the mighty ruins, and the eyes of the audience
are carried to the Orient.

Ann Hathaway's husband lived Every life, in
his imagination.

He lacked the finish of education, but this very
fact made it possible for him to leap beyond
the bounds of the educated.

Education without Capacity, and you have an
empty cask.

This man heard Memnon's morning song,
where marble lips were smitten by a sultry
sun — and all in his vivid Imagination.

He crawled into the narrow cave with the cold
clay of man. Then he resurrected his abnor-
mal mind, and through his lips he whispered
the suffocating doubts of the condemned.

He felt the pangs of every Hell on earth and
in the earth. He pictured the beauties of
every conceivable Heaven here or hereafter.
From the tragic depths of Universal Death to

83

the shallow reefs of Riotous Life, he reflected humans in their every antic, every act.

This man was so many-formed in his mental capacity that he resembled the variety of fast-moving clouds and their constantly changing colorings.

His heart sang all the Songs, and his eyes had been bathed with every bitter Tear. His noons and nights of success and failure were constantly coming, constantly going.

Ann Hathaway's husband had no Equal, nor will he have a Second.

He was "an intellectual ocean whose waves touched all the shores of thought, and from which all rivers, isles and continents of the world of thought receive their dew and rain."

Now let me see if I can make this picture of Ann Hathaway's husband serve you with more than simple interest:

Blessed be the man that finds his distaff, that knows his own spindle. Blessed be the man that Sticks to his Last.

Ann Hathaway's husband Stuck to his Last.

He would have made a poor merchant, an unsuccessful manufacturer or a second-rate salesman.

He found what he Fitted into; and he Stuck to his Job, and made a success of his Job.

And now let us place the emphasis of my point

84

in the right direction:
It is not so much, What do you Want to do?
as What can you Best do?
Life and its successes is wholly a question of Individual Fitness.

The world, in its coming centuries, will have time in which to make discoveries, but you, my friend, have none too much time in which to become Worth Discovering.

In the future the world will require the Qualified.

For what are you Qualified?

You can never be a Shakespeare.

Remembrance is the Rosemary of Life;
kindness to the living is the golden chain
that holds us humans together.
Let us respect the memory of the Dead,
but above all things let us be kind to the
Living.
Give Me the flowers Now.

HOME HAPPINESS

Let's coin a new word: "Sunsense."
Sunsense means that a man sees the
bright spots in Life — has sense enough
to appreciate the Sunshine.

The lidless eye of God is always shining
for this Sunsense man. There is no black
night of despair for him. He sees
pleasure; and it is a pleasure to see him.

The Sunsense man believes in his neighbor, willingly helps his friend, and always
boosts his own town.

His Life is lived out in the open day. If
it should rain, he recognizes the necessity
of water for saving the crops.

The only clouds the Sunsense man can
see are high in the heavens and swiftly
moving on.

In the last act of a beautiful play by a French author, there is a wonderful thought about husbands and wives who forgive. It is this: "Happiness is so precious" (the French author says) "to some of us that, when it is broken, we stoop and gather up the pieces."

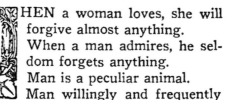

WHEN a woman loves, she will forgive almost anything.

When a man admires, he seldom forgets anything.

Man is a peculiar animal.

Man willingly and frequently forgets the mistakes of a man friend, but he stubbornly refuses to forgive the one that is more than a friend.

It takes a big and a brave man to Forgive the one that is more than a friend. And now the question comes up: Do we expect too much of each other?

Sex to the last, a woman will Hug the offender and Forgive the offense.

A man seems to hold delightful communion with some really forgivable fault and, when defense for his own position is needed, out comes the record, with all its Defects, and is flaunted in the face of the more than friend.

The talent of human nature is to go from one extreme to the other. With this fact always before us, why expect Angels on Earth?

When you want to know just what is in the mind of another, examine closely Your Own Thoughts; for be it known, human nature is more conspicuous for its sameness than for its originality.

In the last act of a beautiful play by a French author, there is a wonderful thought about husbands and wives who forgive. It is this: "Happiness is so precious" (the French author says) "to some of us that, when it is broken, we stoop and gather up the pieces."

THE STAR OF DESTINY

Destiny, the scapegoat which man
makes responsible for all his mishaps.
At least, this was the impression gained
from a talk with N. R. Hopkins, my
friend.

Out West there is a man totally blind.
He is forty-eight years old. He earns his
living by washing windows and scrubbing
floors. He does his work by a system of
mental measurements and a sense of
touch. There is nothing in his work to
indicate his disability.

Milton, Dante, Homer — all blind.

And you, Mr. Reader — well, strong and
living in America with all your friends
— you ask me for help.

What you are, what you hope to be, rests
wholly with you.

Do not plead for a pension; Work for
Prosperity. Blind men do.

Destiny cannot send man anywhere. Thumb over the pages of history and you will find that defeat is nothing but wavering feebleness, or lack of Strength, somewhere, at some vital time.

ESTINY is defined as a pre-determined state. It is Fate; Lot; Doom. Destiny, according to the highest authority, is a resistless power or agency; the Foreordained Future.

Thackeray, Disraeli, Shakespeare, Longfellow, Voltaire and so many more great minds all refer to Destiny.

Goldsmith says: "We are all sure of two things, at least: we shall suffer and we shall all die."

Bryant insists that no man or woman born, coward or brave, can shun his Destiny.

Voltaire writes this thought: "Everything is done by immutable laws, and Destiny is already recorded."

George Eliot asked this question: "Can man or woman choose duties? No more than they can choose their birthplace or their father or mother."

Shakespeare insists: "What Fates impose, that man must needs abide."

In the presence of these great thinkers, marvelous philosophers, you would not expect a small man like me to doubt the irrevocable command of Destiny.

The Buck Up Book emphatically denies, positively contradicts the power of Destiny — the existence of "a resistless power or agency" other than God — and no one worth while will contradict this world-established Truth.

You may ask for bigger and better authority than my word. Let me loan you a thought from Bulwer-Lytton. It seems to be a crushing blow to Destiny:

"It is Destiny — phase of the weak human heart; a dark apology for every error. The strong and the virtuous admit no Destiny. On earth, guides conscience; in heaven, watches God. And Destiny is but the phantom we evoke to silence the one, to dethrone the other."

Destiny cannot send man anywhere. Thumb over the pages of history and you will find that defeat is nothing but wavering feebleness, or lack of Strength, somewhere, at some vital time.

What the author is trying to establish in your mind is this fact; Most humans misconstrue

94

the meaning of the English language.
The author is convinced that the great thinkers employed the word " Destiny " for convenience sake.
They took the poetical license in their teeth and ran away with the word.
They attached too much importance to an Impotent Idea.

When old Noah began building his boat,
the landlubbers, the frog-pond croakers,
called him crazy. They proclaimed that
the ship carpenter was off his base.
Those harpers and critics said old Noah
was a bug.

They said that the very fact he was building an Ark would bring on a flood.
Preparation would start something.

Some time after that, and while Captain
Noah sat on the bow of his boat, his
self-respect seemed to increase, and he
often wondered just what had become of
his Critics.

THE EARNEST MAN

Environment includes so much! Environment is surrounding conditions, forces. When you consider that environment means the aggregate of all external influences, you are certainly taking in some Territory.

Blood may tell a lot, but I have known a peach tree to bear fine plums.

So much can be done with nature and with human nature by grafting!

Never walk with a man who refuses to be large. Rub elbows with the doers of Real things. Steer clear of the dead ones. If you sympathize with dead ones, send them a check, but never let their morbid Influence get under your skin.

No man can improve himself in any society that lacks the restraining influence of self-respect, self-help.

Neither is it best for a man to assemble only with men of his own calling. Get a variety of experiences. It gives you a New Angle on the way you work.

Climb to the tonic mountains of Good Health. Let your heart go high with Hope. Drink deeply of the spring of Inspiration, and steer clear of the back barnyard pool.

Avoid men who Fear and women who are Jealous.

Environment either Energizes or Enervates.

The earnest man sustains hope among his associates, makes light of difficulties, and gives Endurance to those about him.
Blessings on the bean of the Earnest Man!

MEN of enthusiasm are always appointed. We figure them big. Men of enthusiasm are almost always featured, yet I have known many of these men who missed the mark by a mile.

Let us compare enthusiasm with earnestness. The earnest man seldom Fails to find Success. Enthusiasm is a very big word in business, but earnestness is the Passport to permanency. The Silent Partner has great faith in the enthusiastic man and a lot of faith in the Earnest Man.

The earnest man may not achieve the unheard of or the miraculous. He may not overwhelm all obstacles and have a torchlight parade. He may not engulf competition and put it on the blink; but give him sufficient time and equal support, and you will Always find him

99

where you have reason to expect him — On the Job!

There is no virtue so much needed in this world as earnestness.

Single-handed earnestness inspires double-handed co-operation of employees.

One steady, sturdy, honest soul will bring more Success to a business than half a dozen hop, skip and jump members of the organization.

The earnest man helps to pay Dividends. He is the bedrock result getter.

THE MIND AND MEDICINE

Anger is one of man's most flagrant faults. Anger is practical foolishness. Anger is not argument, neither is it an evidence of Power.

Reason is as far from anger as Pottstown is from Potsdam.

Anger is a surface madness and not a down-deep resentment.

Anger is usually the answer to some small displeasure and more often ends in Repentance.

Getting riled, getting provoked, getting incensed and then flying off the handle is a passion that never pays.

Review the results of the past and you will find that all accomplishment worth while was brought about while you were in a mental poise.

Anger poisons the body, queers the nerves, weakens the intellect and withers the Soul.

Getting angry will eventually put the death rattle in your throat. Anger will put a crimp in your cash balance and finally take you from yourself.

Let a man be wrong and fail to admit it, and the very first thing he will do is to get angry.

Anger is outside evidence of inside Weakness.

Anger seldom, if ever, accomplishes its purpose, but always recoils, hits and Hurts the man that loses his Head.

The Mind is Master until — until the Mind, by disease, is mastered. In this very fact we find the necessity of a science that can step in and Nurse and Nourish.

NOAH, the man that made the dictionary, Defines disease as a derangement or disorder of the Mind, of Morals, Character or Habits.

Noah, he took no chances with this word. He covered it from soup to finger bowl.

Noah makes it clear that Disease is an alteration in some function of the body or some of its organs, interrupting or disturbing Health. Webster remains silent on the subject of Morals or Character. Noah builds an Ark of Safety around this subject.

Now that we know what disease is from the highest authority in English, why not consider the word — Cure?

Cure, according to the same authority is restoration of Health from Disease — the means of Removal of Evil.

Here is another opportunity for you to study

103

the word **Cure.** Ask your Curate what it means.

Noah next tells us that the Mind is Memory, Recollection — that the Mind is a mental mood, cast of thought or feeling. He tells us that " Mind Cure " is a method or act of healing Disease by Mental Action.

Obviously the question of Disease as related to Cure and the Mind has some real reason for serious consideration.

Shakespeare has this to say: " By medicine life may be prolonged, yet death will seize the doctor too."

It is my impression that William paid an unintentional tribute to the doctor.

Longfellow reasons in this manner: " Joy, temperance and repose shove the door on the doctor's nose."

Again my contention is that the physician is a profoundly Important Factor in the life and the health of humans.

The man who studies nature closely and for a long time, the man who understands clearly the diseases that assail the human body, the man who knows the properties of the human body and the remedies that will benefit it deserves much More Credit in this world than he gets.

In event of the physician's making a mistake,

104

the earth, in its mercy, covers it up.

You can never get me even to try to discount the physician.

It was O. W. Holmes who often went a mile past the bounds of reason while clinging closely to a fine phrase.

More than once, Holmes hit a high spot, and here is one: "I firmly believe that if the whole materia medica could be sunk to the bottom of the sea, it would be all the better for mankind and all the worse for the fishes."

Holmes was right. Most men and nearly all women take too much Dope.

A wound will mend much sooner if the Mind is hopeful, cheerful.

Under no circumstances allow your mind to dwell on Self-sympathy.

Let me give you a true story of a soldier who was about to die: The hospital physician had given up all hope. Suddenly it occurred to the soldier that he could not afford to die and leave his Wife and two Babies without funds.

This responsibility braced him, and his resolve saved him. He decided not to die. He made up his Mind to help the doctor, and he did. The doctor could then help him, and he did.

The great business of a man is, after all, to

Manage his Mind in such a way that his body will steer clear of contagion; that his Nerves will not be taxed beyond their endurance; that his Belly will not be expected to hold two quarts of indigestibles — Ice and Intoxicants. Witness the marvelous influence of the Mind over the body — the sublime dominion when, for a time, the Mind can make flesh and nerves impregnable, make the body strong and the sinews like steel, make a frail body like a bridge of almost Unaccountable Strength.

Witness the tens of thousands of Disciplined Minds — Minds of intelligent individuals of unquestionable integrity, who believe that medicine is Never necessary, and on this belief they hinge their hope of Living.

Old Cicero hit the bull's-eye too. Listen: " The diseases of the mind are more and more destructive than those of the body."

And now we are coming to My Real Thought: The Mind is Master until — until the Mind, by disease, is mastered. In this very fact we find the necessity of a science that can step in and Nurse and Nourish.

And here the author leaves you with several thoughts on the Mind and Medicine.

BE SURE

Every organization has its Mr. Put-it-off-skie.

The recruiting officer of the Army of Failures is officially called "Put-it-off-skie."

To-morrow (when you reach it) will be yesterday, if you fail to do the thing that day.

I have watched many men work, and this watching process and my own disposition have taught me that a large number of good men pay dues to the Do-it-later Club.

Putting off important things not only steals time, but it clogs the Wheels of Business.

Business, to be a success, must be done on regular schedule — service must be performed on time.

The mere delay of a day may not cost in cash very much, but who knows when or where to Depend on the man that Delays?

BEFORE you begin, be sure of your ground. Napoleon made his mistake, and he Paid the Price because he did not know his ground.

Napoleon trusted to a guide, and when Lacoste answered " No," Napoleon ordered Milhaud's cuirassiers ahead.

What a frightful moment!

There was the ravine, unlooked for, yawning for the bodies of fifteen hundred men and two thousand horses.

There was a living grave, two fathoms deep, with double slopes.

Victor Hugo, in his description of " The Battle of Waterloo," says: " The second rank, the third pushed in, Horses reared, fell upon their backs and struggled with their feet in the air; no hope, no chance was there for retreat. The whole living mass of men and animals was a terrible projectile."

The only force left to Crush the English annihilated itself.

The inexorable ravine could not yield until it was filled. The riders and horses rolled in together pell-mell, grinding each other, making common flesh in this dreadful gulf; and when the grave was full of living and dead, the rest Rode Over them and passed on.

The lesson we learn from this thought is this: Accustom yourself to make doubly sure on Every Occasion that the way is clear ahead before you charge.

In the womb of to-morrow there may be some Obstacle yet unborn that you are to encounter.

It is your duty as a Leader to know the way is open before you go ahead.

Lacoste was a good guide until the battle of Waterloo.

GREAT MEN

Discipline is the development of the faculties by Instruction and Exercise. It is training, whether it be physical, mental or moral.

The habit of Obedience to the demands of life is of supreme importance.

Discipline may seem stern and cruel, but this is why Discipline is eventually so very kind.

Lack of discipline has filled our jails, crowded our poorhouses and littered the lowlands of life with many men that might have made good.

Obedience is the combination that unlocks success. The first great Law commands us to Obey.

The truth is, the only real Liberty is founded in Obedience.

When a man Obeys the commands of his superior officer he finds no time to dispute the plans.

Obedience is the universal Duty and Destiny.

The great men of yesterday were great because the people of their day were on their knees.

T is a general expression or conclusion that all great men are Dead.

This is a mistake, Some of the greatest are now Living — men whose greatness will only be exceeded by the greatness to come.

It is a mistake to go about tearing down old tombstones in order to locate great men.

One of the greatest dangers of modern America is a tendency to make Miracles out of Past Works and belittle or criticize Present Achievements.

The results accomplished in this war will be looked upon by coming generations as the Most Marvelous in the history of man.

Why worship at the tomb of Cæsar? Why weep at the place where the ashes of Solomon are scattered?

If the more recent results of Schwab, Ford,

113

DuPont do not make the memories of the dead old ones — or the old dead ones — look like counterfeit coin, my measure of value is a mile off.

The old tops of long ago were Long on whiskers and Short on electric lights, automobiles and the wireless.

It is enough to make a man laugh to think of comparing some of our modern men and their Achievements with the old guys who wore a G string for an evening dress.

If the "great men" of long ago were so very great, why did they hold up their sleeves so many Necessary Inventions?

The great men of yesterday were great because the people of their day were on their knees.

THE SUREST WAY

The truest opinion concerning my Manners will always come from my enemy — that is, if I take pains to drain off what I know to be Prejudice.

Therefore, my enemy is my necessary Friend — more than a friend; for a friend will flatter you into a False opinion of yourself.

Making a success of Life and making a success in life are two vastly different viewpoints.

HE surest way to avoid Failure is to determine Not to fail.

The only way that you can Succeed permanently is to work out the details of your Determination, intelligently, industriously.

I am not referring to the glare and dazzle of dollars, the success that makes fools admired or the success that throws a veil over the evil deeds of men and their manners.

My measure of success is a series of small but legitimate results that contribute to the good of society and to the good of Oneself.

If you aspire to make money rapidly; if it is your ambition to speculate into success, The Buck Up Book will be of no service to you.

Real success is a result of slow growth.

Few men are willing to pay the price of real success — Patience.

Real success has no special trade, no particular

117

business, no select profession.

What may be considered by one man to be a success, is often measured by another man as a failure. Real success cannot be weighed on the scales of cold cash.

Life is a success. Death is a failure unless you have made a success of Life.

Making a success of Life and making a success in life are two vastly different viewpoints. What will it profit you to make a million in cash, if, while piling up a few carloads of clamshells, you get hit with the Indian sign of locomotor ataxia?

The possession of the greatest god below the sky — money — is an advantage when it serves society and serves the individual faithfully and well.

The largest slaveholder in all the world is the wretched, impotent, shining metal — Gold.

Big men, great men, do not work for mere pay. Men like M. L. Parker, of Davenport, plan and persevere for the supreme satisfaction of making a success, not for the mere empty reward of making money.

Little men see success in a big bank roll, and these little men make a failure out of life in their frantic efforts to get money honestly — if they Can — but to get money even though they must " Can " honestly.

118

Money is necessary. So is dirt.
The value of a dollar is comparative. It is
more to the world when it pays for education
than when it buys booze. It is more in some
men's hands than it is in others.
Money is a Means and not a Measure of Success.

Health is wealth, and good cheer is cash on hand.

The real millionaire is the man who can smile and mean it.

The most useful, the most successful, men in this country have the happy faculty of Smiling, and then saying something Cheerful.

I do not mean the grin-smile — the smile that the lion wears when he had found a way of exit — the smile that is as grateful as a dissolving cake of ice.

I mean the smile that looks like sunshine when sunshine breaks through the storm clouds on a morning in May.

DIED WITHOUT THINKING

Good Humor is the clear, blue sky of the soul. Good Humor is good sense, for cheerfulness is health and the opposite is disease — melancholy.

The most manifest sign of good health and a good heart is continued cheerfulness.

The grouch is the guy that gets your goat.

If you want to locate the man with kindness in his heart and sympathy in his soul, pause when you bump up against the good-natured, good-humored human.

Good Humor is the bright weather of the heart.

Cheerful, hopeful people refresh you. Why not render an extra effort to confer the blessings of Good Humor on the other fellow?

Here he lies! Dead he is not, but departed—
for the provident man Never dies.

O man will stand and stare at
the fierce light of a burning
sun. Few men can be cor-
nered and made to look
straight into their own Con-
sciences.
But I've got you, Friend Reader; got you
where I want you; got you before the infallible
court of Conscience; got you in the presence
of the always reliable counsel; got you in the
chamber of Real justice — got you where you
must listen to the still, small voice of Conscience.

Conscience is more than a mere spiritual suggestion — more than a moral law. Conscience invades the realm of Individual Responsibility.

Conscience is a clock whose hands are constantly pointing to the ever-changing hours
for improving your position in life. Conscience is a clock that strikes the hour to do a

thing — that has the alarm that awakens at the right hour.

This very hour, Friend Reader, has arrived.

If Death should open the Great Gate and beckon you in, what would you do, or what would you be willing to do?

You would willingly, if it were possible, give all you have for another Hour in which to close up some important matters — to obey the dictates of your own Conscience.

When Death beckons, you are carried in without a chance to compromise.

Knowing this, why do you Hesitate?

You have an immediate duty to perform, a positive work to carry out, and your Conscience indicates that I am telling the truth.

And now to the point: Death is not the terrible thunder that follows the formidable flash. When you hear the thunder you are safe.

You have heard my words, and your Conscience reaffirms this truth: The man who has not neglected to provide for his family, after his death, leaves this thought for an epitaph:

Here he lies! Dead he is not, but departed — for the provident man Never dies.

Better your name be written in water than have it said: He Died Without Thinking of hose he left behind.

UNCONSCIOUSLY MEASURED

Pope says: "Act well your part, here all honor lies."

So many men and so many women seem to think that one must hold a prominent position in life to be entitled to the epaulet of honor — that they must wear the soldier's uniform!

The little girl behind the counter, the overgrown boy on the delivery wagon, the man in overalls and jumper, or the woman who wears calico Deserves honor. Then again, folks are inclined to look upon people who have political honor as in a position to be envied. Political honor is often as insecure, unstable, as that of public opinion upon which political honor feeds.

To those who render faithful and efficient service in some worthy work, I say all Honor.

Honor is empty unless based on moral conscience and honest toil.

To the salespeople of this country who are true to themselves, to the competent stenographers or secretaries, to the engineers and firemen, to the farmers, and to everybody, let me repeat the line of Pope: "Act well your part, here all honor lies."

PERSISTENCY is the thing that Wins more than any other one thing.

It often matters little about the pole, the line, the hook. Sometimes the fish bite without bait.

The postage stamp will stick only after you lick it.

It is the steady sticking that carries a man where he wants to go.

The power of purpose, the bulldog tenacity, the stick-to-it-iveness of a man is not always a good pattern to go by; but I am not considering the morals of a man in this article. I am just emphasizing the absolute Necessity of sticking to a job until you Finish — of getting Home from Third.

In a solitary cell, a life convict drew strings from his woolen socks, soaked these strings with his spittle, and then rubbed these wet

127

strings with grit from the prison floor.   After three years of continuous, steady sawing with these slender strings, he wore away a prison bar and Escaped.

In a respectable way, in a legitimate business, are you ready and willing to make this tremendous effort to free yourself from Imprisonment?

All great accomplishments have been performed by Perseverance rather than by ability.

And this thought opens the Great Gate for every man or every woman in America.

What you lack is Ambition — nine times out of ten.

If you were to ask me to tell you the Royal Road to Success, my answer would be: It's blocked.

This sounds rather discouraging until you analyze my thought.

Do you want to go over a "royal road?"

Europe is lined with "royal roads."

If you would know the Rough Road to Permanent Success, here is my answer: Do the First thing First, and then keep right on Doing.

THRIFT

If you have in mind some one thing that you would like to accomplish, some position that you would like to fill, remember the Creator did not make a mind capable of planning and of understanding, without hands competent to mold these thoughts into material form.

The Temple of Thrift should stand on the campus at the left of the College and at the right of the Chapel.

N my desk lies a line drawing — a picture of a provident man descending the stone steps of a savings bank. Evidently this man is of middle age, of moderate means, healthy and Honest. His head is erect, his shoulders square, and his general appearance indicates individual Worth. The suggestion in this picture is that this man has just left a certain sum in the savings bank.

At the foot of the stone steps, and in the shelter of the great granite pillar, stands a cringing, half-clad, pitifully poor man. His eyes stare, his face is haggard, and he looks cold and hungry. Poverty has snuffed out every spark of success in this man, and made him Desperate. He is a rudderless, hopeless, helpless Derelict.

And the interesting part of this situation is that both men started out in early Life with equal advantages; both men came from the same little town.

One began to save, and the other began to spend. Both, for a time, earned the same salary.

Finally the spender was compelled to dodge the tailor, the grocer and the butcher. Eventually this man began to lose Self-Confidence, later he lost his Pride, and then he lost his Position.

How he spent his money, or where he spent it, is not my point. He Spent it, and that is enough.

The other man continually Saved a little, and then a little more; and finally this habit of saving was permanently formed. Eventually this man placed a little money out at interest, and his money began to Work for him.

At last the man with the saving habit became what we call " comfortably well off."

Now, friend reader, there is nothing sensational, nothing unreasonable, nothing Uncommon in a man's becoming " comfortably well off." Nor is there anything uncommon in a man's going broke.

This picture is not overdrawn. It is not necessary to overdraw a picture of this character.

There are Millions of men — clever men — who are mentally unfit, physically unclean,

and morally out of position, due to Improvi-
dence.

Money is the measure of food, of clothing, of
the necessities of life; and the man who fails
to look out for to-morrow is Dishonest with
himself, Unfair to his family, and will eventually Fail.

Saving is more than saving: it more often
proves a Saving Grace.

Too much money, or too little money, is a
sorry situation that can be met successfully
only by Sensible men.

Give the average young man plenty of money
to start with, and you handicap him. Give
a young man with ambition an opportunity,
and then teach him to save money, and you
have laid the foundation for a Permanent
Success.

Success all depends on how you start. If
you begin at the bottom and build on your
profit, on what you Save, you are creating a
combination of character, capital and com-
mercial worth that is of Tremendous Importance.

If you begin at the top of the ladder, without
experience, but with plenty of inherited capital,
make up your mind that sooner or later you
will see the box where they Mix the Mortar.
Personal Extravagance has encompassed

more Defeats than anything I know of. Prudence points the way to Prosperity.

The improvident, careless, reckless, thoughtless man is a Personal Failure and a tax on others.

Show me the man with the " saving " habit, and I will point to you an Honest Man.

If the night courts and the day courts are crowded with men charged with all the crimes on the calendar, and if nine men out of ten in these courts are poverty-poor, broken in pocketbook, broken in Spirit, what does this situation suggest?

Men are naturally honest. It is the spur of old Necessity, the poverty-prod of Want, that prompts men to take chances. Necessity and Want are not the natural offspring of the habit of Saving.

Poverty lashes a man to the wild horse of Don't Care. Want whispers in the ear of a weakling and tells him to take a Chance.

Money in the savings bank gives a man Credit in a community — self-confidence.

Ownership multiplies the ambition for more. Poverty Paralyzes Purpose. I am invariably stronger with, than without, money.

In any organization the individual who is forever borrowing money is constantly exhibiting a lack of that something which made the boss a Success.

The Mind cannot work well if fearing failure or seeing sickness and the dreaded doctor's bill. The Mind, to do its Best work, must be Free from fretting and the frenzied attacks of Want.

Take two men. Give them both an equal chance. Have one Save money each week. Have the other Spend all that he earns, and perhaps more. Which man will Produce the better Results?

The man who saves a little money each week also saves his energy. He comes to the store, to the plant, or goes out on the road, with his Mind Right and his Body Right.

The man who is compelled to rob a child's bank for carfare is committing no crime, but he is skating mighty close to a Bad Habit — robbing a bank.

Men are creatures of habit. They contract certain customs. They are apt to follow the line of Least Resistance, and to get into a groove, a rut. They keep on in the old jog-trot way until they get seasoned to Failure!

The greatest instrument of good and the most convenient tool for evil is the tongue. The tongue is what gets us in bad. When you hold your tongue, you hold the respect and confidence of the wise.

Lincoln said little, and Grant said less. When some gabber would gab, walk in the direction of silence; take up your tent and move where it's quiet. You can't think when the other fellow's tongue hangs on a swivel. So, you see, the tongue has a lot to do with other than the talker.

Washington talked only when necessary. Napoleon was as silent as a steam calliope with a broken boiler.

Silent men Do things. Talkers undo.

The more you talk, the less time you have to Think — the less time others have to Think.

A CARELESS EPITAPH

If you start to explore, you are sure to find yourself at the end of some unknown lane, footsore, weary.

If you have the good luck to get lost, you are sure to learn the character of the country as a result of your wanderings.

Knowledge comes from getting off the track, from making mistakes.

Make mistakes — but Never make the same mistake twice.

Carelessness is inexcusable. It is either disinterest of the Heart or disqualification of the Head.

RIENDS have asked me to write an epitaph on the man that is Careless. And, strange to say, the man for whom the epitaph is to be written still lives, still walks in freedom, while the didn't-know-it-was-loaded victim is as dead as yesterday.

The careless man has danced down the ages with his blindfolded eyes, and as far as I am personally concerned he is as Dead as the leaves on a painted canvas.

I would rather live in a henhouse, and be compelled to claw and paw for a position on the roosting pole at night, than have a careless employee in my organization and be compelled to continue his or her employment.

Carelessness is inexcusable. It is either disinterest of the Heart or disqualification of the Head.

139

In other words, a good fellow can become No Good by simply being careless.

The careless loom up on locomotives and on the ledger; they are found in factories and supported in stores.

You can watch the dishonest, guide the ignorant, coax or drive the lazy; but the careless man is the lukewarm loon that looks like a Man, walks like a Man — but he " ain't."

Every organization has the individual who " didn't mean to do it "— has the slob who " didn't think," and says so after he costs the company a lot of money and perhaps a Life or two.

Careless people seldom have anything to give to make good for their brain-sick mistakes; so you see how explosive, how expensive, they are.

And now for the Epitaph: .

The individual that is Careless is as impossible as mending a broken bell; impractical as to attempt to satisfy a hungry lion with a club sandwich; impotent as the dead past, and as Inefficient as a safety razor at a negro ball.

A TIP ON COURTSHIP

You cannot reason in a rage. You cannot balance your mental faculties when swinging in Suspense. You cannot win when you are Worried. You cannot calculate intelligently while Doubting your own position.

You cannot accumulate while compelled to discount a limited income; you cannot borrow, beg, bow, and win.

Quarreling, fighting, passion unfit you. Trouble, jealousy, worry unnerve you. Poverty, pessimism and pleading paralyze you. To Win, a man must enjoy the full measure of every faculty; have peace, comfort and real mental and physical rest in his home. He must have help from his Home.

Take away the inspiration of home and its energizing environs, remove this moral influence, and you have weighed anchor in the face of a gale.

Don't tell the present girl too much about the past ladies. She may give you credit for knowing too much.

HE man who has never had a Courtship is as blind as a bat; while right before his sightless eyes you will find running a beautiful river, and on its banks you will see long-stemmed American beauties all blushing because they cannot conceal their bare feet.

If you get a chance to court a girl, by all means court her; don't Flunk.

If you stand on the bank and shiver, you will be twice as cold as the chap who takes a Deep Dive and later tells you the water is warm.

Courting is like the dry-goods business: Next season the entire color scheme of dress goods may change, and who wants to wear a Remnant?

Always court a girl as you eat ice cream. Take your Time and get the full Flavor.

Fail to enjoy a couple of seasons of courting,

and you can never hope to know what Heaven is until you go hence.

Courting a girl reminds me of two rivulets that come dancing down the mountain side, side by side. They dash along, dance and murmur, sing and splash each other. They go foaming, frothing, cascading, hiding here and there; and all the way, to them, it's down hill. It's first shadows, then sunshine, until at last they Meet and Join — and then they go slowly.

And here is the crux of this chapter on Courting: Don't tell the present girl too much about the past ladies. She may give you credit for Knowing too much.

LOST IN THE MOB

A crowbar will loosen the bulldog's grip, but a common mongrel lets his own jaw slip. A little man lives on what he calls "Luck," the big man on what we call "Pluck."

Big men never recognize Luck, but they do accept Law.

THE singular thing in life is this: All opposition seems to lose its substance the moment we grapple with it in real earnest.

Benjamin Franklin wheeled all the material he had, to start a printing plant — wheeled, through the streets of Philadelphia, to his sleeping room, which was his office, all the tools he had.

Just as soon as he got his plant located, he called his formidable competitor to his "office," and this is about what he said: "If you can sleep on a board, live on a crust and drink water as a beverage, you can hope to destroy my plans for printing a newspaper." Mention the name of Napoleon, and Fresh Resolution, great promise of performance, wonderful personal vigor present themselves. Sound the name of Pershing, and a spark suddenly develops into a flame of "I will."

The big rewards of life are given not to the man who goes the greater distance, but to the man who overcomes the greater handicap.

Providence puts in a man's path Hazards and Handicaps — not to punish the man, but to Prepare the man.

Suffering, storms, hostilities, disaster are all dealt out to try the mettle of the man, to rouse the man's faculties, to school his passions.

Temptations and trials are but part of a liberal education. When the world hands you one of its rude jolts, accept the discipline as a chapter in the Book of Knowledge.

Never for one instant lean back and declare that you are out of Luck!

Big men never recognize Luck, but they do accept Law.

The big man considers wisely, resolves firmly, executes with inflexible purpose — and executes promptly.

The small man hesitates, trusts to Luck — and is lost in the Mob!

THE LONG PROMISER

It is perfectly natural for some people to be constantly telling their troubles. For the moment, these sympathy solicitors get reserved seats in our hearts, but after they move on we cannot help feeling that they are Weak and Selfish.

Every man has his own fish to fry; every person his own web to weave, his own struggles, difficulties, handicaps. We all find stubborn, trying, refractory situations.

Few men care to listen to the other fellow's troubles.

There is no clear sailing for anybody. There are quicksands, breakers, shoals, for all of us.

Every human is beset with critical, ticklish, embarrassing, perplexing difficulties. Tell your troubles to the chattering monkeys in the zoo.

If you want to please another, do something
Worth While and then deliver the worth-while
something and let the receiver do the talking.

LONG, long before this, you have met the Long-Promiser. The long-promiser is omnipresent. The woods are full of him. The Long-Promiser is the individual that is always going to do something for you some time in the near future.

A Long-Promiser seldom performs. He is like a false fire to an old-fashioned cannon — it dischargeth a good expectation with a bad report.

It is adding insult to injury to promise something and then fail to produce, unless — unless you have a Good Excuse.

A long promise sounds like bullycon. Why underwrite some understanding unless you mean to carry it through? Why promise a friend anything? Do the thing for a friend and then the promise is unnecessary.

A long promise is pretty poor evidence of down-deep sincerity to serve.

If you want to please another, do something worth while, and then deliver the worth-while something and let the receiver do the talking. I have, at the moment, a man in mind that collects a check of me every month for a service that is indeed small. Just before the regular time for this check I always get a "hint," and accompanying this hint, as a postscript, is a long promise, either with words or in writing. My Long-Promiser friend promises he will do something for me very soon.

Do something? Leached lime and tobacco dust! Fertilizer!

WHEN WE WERE BOYS

In order to do constructive work, a human must have an individual incentive — must be personally interested in the enterprise, in the effort on hand.

This is a law of human nature, and when you run contrary to human nature you spill the beans.

Work is not what some folks think it is. Work is an opportunity by which you are expected to show what you can actually accomplish.

People are paid to-day on a basis of results and not on a basis of long Promises, long Pedigrees or a strong Pull.

It is not my purpose to turn the Leaves of Memory to a page of the Past, where naught but dead garlands cover the mounds. It is my plan to bring back Boyhood's Happy Days.

IME, with its wings, flies on insensibly and so deceives us that we are compelled to pause in order to really understand how long ago it was that we were boys.

It is not my purpose to turn the Leaves of Memory to a page of the Past, where naught but dead garlands cover the mounds. It is my plan to bring back Boyhood's Happy Days.

Let me take you back to the pioneer pleasures that we freckle-faced boys enjoyed. Back to the time when James Whitcomb Riley was a boy, back to when the frost was on the "punkin"— back to "when we ust to be so happy and so pore."

Let me take you back in your memory to the new-mown hay. Back to the fields of clover. Back to the frost-cracked chestnuts and the fire-cracked yellow corn.

155

Yes, let's you and I go back to the time when
Riley "ust" to be so happy and so "pore."
And here is the way to take you back — back
to the days when you were a lad and would
look through the back lots for two hours on a
cold September morn; barefoot — look for
that blamed brindle cow that was lost.
I can see, in my memory, Guilford R. Adams
dressed in knee pants — pants held by one
single denim-strap suspender slung over his
left shoulder — a big Responsibility on a
shingle-nail fastner.
And this reminds me of a bit of verse that I
saw recently:

Two ladies gay met a boy one day.
  His legs were briar-scratched;
His clothes were blue, but a nut-brown hue
  Marked the place where his pants were
      patched.
They bubbled with joy at the blue-clad boy,
  With his spot of nut-brown hue.
"Why didn't you patch with a color to
     match?"
  They chuckled; "Why not in blue?
Come, don't be coy, my blue-brown boy,
  Speak out," and they laughed with glee.
And he blushed rose-red while he bashfully
     said:
  "That ain't no patch; that's me!"

156

AFTERWORD

MERSON said: "No sensible person ever made an apology."

It is the author's contention that few explanations explain —that an apology is an acknowledgment of some shortcoming.

It is not my intention to apologize for the sincere frankness of this book. Those who understand my motives will consider an apology unnecessary.

Those who regard my work as brutally blunt will never forgive me; so why justify or apologize, why try to justify?

In presenting this effort to encourage, to enthuse — to get humans to think up, brush up, Buck Up — there is no necessity for defense. The book is its own defense.

Every line in this work was written with a smile in the author's heart for You.

So let's shake hands and always be Friends.

THE SILENT PARTNER
SCRAP BOOK

THE SILENT PARTNER SCRAP BOOK is a choice selection of the thoughts you would like to take with you down into the Valley of Time.

I have tried, in THE SILENT PARTNER SCRAP BOOK, to crowd between its covers every evidence possible of my most earnest and enthusiastic work.

It's a pleasure-bearing, radiant, genial remembrance that will last long after my name is forgotten: for I have not tried to make this book ME; I have battled to make it all YOU.

THE SILENT PARTNER SCRAP BOOK contains about forty articles, including "What is Holding You Back?" (over a million copies of this article have been printed), and "The Rosary," where both kissed the cross.

To sum it all up in a few words, I believe that the deeper the convictions, the firmer the beliefs, the less it is necessary to demonstrate, by an expression of these beliefs, these convictions. For this reason, I will ask you to believe me when I say that THE SILENT PARTNER SCRAP BOOK is a book that you will be proud of.

F. D. VAN AMBURGH,

The Author.

Done de luxe, limp-leather binding, deckle-edged, gilt top, printed in two colors, mailed in a suitable box, all for $2.50.

Done in cloth, gilt name, printed in two colors, deckle-edged, mailed in a paper box, all for $1.25.

Remember: Not sold by dealers — By mail only.

Address: Van Amburgh (The Silent Partner), 200 Fifth Avenue, New York City.

BY THE SIDE
OF THE ROAD

BY THE SIDE OF THE ROAD is a book in which I have tried
to bring back the sunbeams of the South, the snow-caps of the
North, the teeming marts of the crowded East and the great hills
of the vast Alone.

In this book I have tried to make my thoughts bigger and broader
than any single street — tried to touch the Octaves in human
Activities and the lost chord in Human Hearts.

Briefly, I have tried to give expression to the thoughts that will
work in Everyday Life — thoughts that will help humans up the
hill. I have tried to introduce enough Enthusiasm and Energy,
with words, to make the book wanted. And then it was all bound
with the lavender ribbon of Remembrance and Good Will.

Over forty subjects — including two particular subjects that have
stood the acid Test of Time: " December," an article that deals
with the great Emotions of Life; and the subject, " His Mother,"
a lofty appreciation of the author's intended tribute to a Grand
Old Woman.

F. D. VAN AMBURGH,
The Author.

Done de luxe, limp-leather binding, deckle-edged, gilt top, printed
in two colors, mailed in a suitable box, all for $2.50.

Done in cloth, gilt name, printed in two colors, deckle-edged,
mailed in a paper box, all for $1.25.

Remember: Not sold by dealers — By mail only.

Address: Van Amburgh (The Silent Partner),
200 Fifth Avenue, New York City.

THE BUCK UP BOOK

THE BUCK UP BOOK is before you. In style of binding, printing and general make-up it is an exact pattern of THE SILENT PARTNER SCRAP BOOK (see announcement on previous page). THE BUCK UP BOOK is an exact mechanical reproduction of my other book, BY THE SIDE OF THE ROAD (see announcement on previous page).

Books published by Van Amburgh (The Silent Partner) are not sold by book dealers or by book agents. All books must be ordered direct from The Silent Partner Company.

THE BUCK UP BOOK is for humans who have taken the wrong fork in the road; for those who have wandered into the cemetery of lost Hope, looking for the marker of an almost forgotten Friend. This book is written to the Discouraged — to the dried, cold hearts of humans who are trying to Begin Again.

THE BUCK UP BOOK is to get you to forget self-pity, to cause you to stop wishing, and to go to fishing. It is to get you to look up, think up, brush up, Buck Up, and in this condition you will be able to keep up.

It is trying, with words, to get you to advertise that you are a success, for remember this: Whatever you think you are worth, is about what the world will pay.

F. D. VAN AMBURGH,
The Author.

Done de luxe, limp-leather binding, deckle-edged, gilt top, printed in two colors, mailed in a suitable box, all for $2.50.

Done in cloth, gilt name, printed in two colors, deckle-edged, mailed in a paper box, all for $1.25.

Remember: Not sold by dealers — By mail only.

Address: Van Amburgh (The Silent Partner),
200 Fifth Avenue, New York City.

CPSIA information can be obtained at www.ICGtesting.com
Printed in the USA
BVOW04s0251120615

404363BV00017B/98/P